Three Days in the Light

Blessings for Our Lives

Infinite Light Publishing, LLC
5142 Hollister Ave, #115
Santa Barbara, CA 93111
info@infinitelightpublishing.com

ISBN: 978-0-9884537-4-6 (hardcover) ISBN: 978-0-9884537-5-3 (e-book)

Publisher's Cataloging-in-Publication Data

Sullivan, Ayn Cates.
   Three Days In The Light / Ayn Cates Sullivan ; illustrations by Belle Crow duCray. –
rev. and updated ed.
      pages cm
   Includes index.
   ISBN: 978-0-9884537-4-6 (hardcover)
   ISBN: 978-0-9884537-5-3 (e-book)
   1. Consciousness—Miscellanea. 2. Spiritual life. 3. Self-actualization (Psychology)—
Poetry. 4. Self-realization—Poetry.   I. duCray, Belle Crow, ill. II. Title.
PS3619.U41 U56 2014
811—dc23
[LCCN]

Original Artwork: Belle Crow duCray
Cover Illustration: Lucinda Rae Kinch
Editor: Ken Zeiger
Graphic Design: Isaac Hernández

First Edition 10 9 8 7 6 5 4 3 2 1
Printed in USA

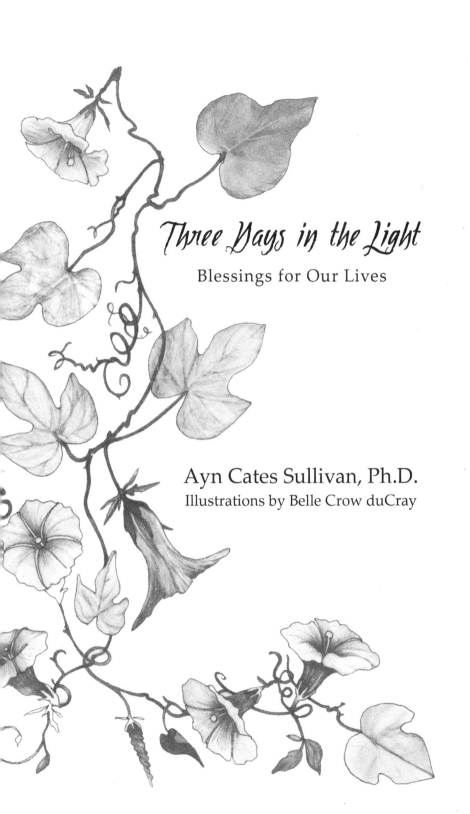

Three Days in the Light

Blessings for Our Lives

Ayn Cates Sullivan, Ph.D.

Illustrations by Belle Crow duCray

Also by Ayn Cates Sullivan Ph.D.

A Story of Becoming
Sparkle & The Light
Sparkle & The Gift
Windhorse: Poems Of Illumination
Consider This: Recovering Harmony & Balance Naturally
Tracking The Deer

www.ayncatessullivan.com

For more information and bulk orders, please contact
publisher: info@infinitelightpublishing.com

To my beloved husband
John Patrick Sullivan,
the journey of awakening is even
more beautiful with you

Contents

4. My Sacred Other

5. The Unbridled Self

6. Like A Gentle River

7. I Am That

Foreword
By Mark Whitwell

Ayn Cates Sullivan's words are English language mantras. They are vibrations of truth. Please make use of them. They will empower your life. For example, just take the title of this book, sit quietly, and repeat it aloud, softly, or silently. See what happens! Or recite just the contents titles one after the other. There is something potent in this for you. And then you have the treasure of each poem if you want to indulge further in the real. Hallelujah!

These utterances from Ayn have come out of her deep abiding in reality itself, that which beats the heart and moves our breath and sex. These words are spoken from her heart, the nurturing source of her life and all of life. You will discover this reality to be your own. You may find that words flow out of your heart too, into your mind and all your relationships.

There is something useful here because Ayn has relaxed so deeply into life that the fire of life has burned up all the suffering that society has put in us. There is no other way, and this can happen for you too. Life burns and throws out of our system every thing that is not needed for our wellness. We can participate consciously in this process as Ayn has. We can build a big bonfire and let it burn! It is known in the Great Tradition of human wisdom that those who have gone from restriction to freedom are very useful to everyone else. They are the best teachers to observe and help us understand our own process. So please listen to these words.

Furthermore, Ayn and her partner John Patrick have taken on sincerely the understanding that when you are connected and sensitive to your own life then you can be intimate with another. I have observed over the years the miracle and power of the relationship between Ayn and John Patrick. They embraced the true meaning of the wisdom: "In the union of opposites we know the source of opposites." The union of opposites is "God's method on Earth," and this is how we know God. They have healed in their own case all the negativity and denial that mankind has created of male female. Ayn and John Patrick have brought dignity and graciousness to their union as an utterly life positive celebration. They have done this for themselves and for all future generations. They have even healed for the past generations who are now gratefully cheering them on. Thank you, Ayn AND John Patrick. Again, Hallelujah!

Three Days in the Light

My greatest longing for two decades, and perhaps for thousands of lifetimes before that, has been to intimately know and understand the intelligence and love that sustains life. By the time the opportunity came along, I was quite content. That had not always been the case, for like many mystics I had struggled with doubt and endured many dark nights. Even when I felt lost I intuitively knew that the first step to true transformation is the willingness to turn our face back to a higher power. The path we follow is less important than the unquenchable desire to find our way Home. For twenty years I prayed, meditated, followed a variety of diets, studied religions, read spiritual poetry, spent time with saints and sages. It is one thing to study God and it is simply pure grace to have a direct experience.

When I met Howard Wills, I had been engaged in deep spiritual practices for a long time. In our first long distance meeting he healed me of chronic asthma. A few months later I injured my hip while riding my horse and when I came to meet him in person he walked out into the living room of the yogi's house where he was working. He was tall and well built with long hair that flowed down his back, and a special blue light seemed to flow from his eyes. He looked at me and said, "Why, you're an angel; you don't want to experience pain anymore, do you?"

I agreed and with the snap of a finger my body re-aligned. My husband and I laughed with delight and asked him how we would spend the hour-long appointment we had scheduled. I told him that I was ready to let go of any story, belief, thought, or misdeed that kept me bound to illusion and falsehood, so that I might know the Infinite Light more fully. With a twinkle in his eyes, Howard suggested that my husband and I hold hands and in his words, "Take it to the next level!"

One day while walking along the beach with Howard, he turned to me and said, "Do you know that God is your best friend?" As I looked into his eyes I simply knew that his words were true and I nodded in agreement, then looked down, for my eyes were filled with tears. I knew that this was a profound moment and one I had been seeking for many years. After working with Howard Wills for about eighteen months on a fairly regular basis, including two personal retreats in Kauai, I became increasingly accustomed to living in alignment with the Infinite Light. My face was turned toward God and the Divine had become my main focus and station. Although I may be described as a religious scholar, I do not consider myself a religious person but a spiritual being having a human experience.

"Go look at your eyes in the mirror," Howard said with his lovely southern drawl. "You're ready to have what you always wanted."

Gazing into the mirror I saw my eyes as reservoirs of a cosmic mystery more vast than I could ever understand. Yet it seemed to me that there was still a veil that kept me from the ultimate truth. I walked back and said to Howard, "What I want most of all is to know God, to completely and fully know the Infinite Light."

Howard smiled and told me that he felt that I was ready. He instructed me to drive home to Ojai and meanwhile spoke with my husband John Patrick about what he might expect. My husband is a yogi and initiated into the mysteries. I was excited and my frequency must have been very high from tapping the cosmic realms because when I touched the ignition button in my car the battery died. This was a new car and when the AAA repairman came he looked puzzled and said, "Your car seems to have had a heart attack from too much energy. Its system is fried."

I almost laughed, but instead apologized to my car for not grounding myself. This was not the first time I had destroyed an electronic device with a touch. It is a running lighthearted joke with my family that I am not allowed to sleep near a computer or security system. Eventually my car was mended and I drove home.

That night a vivid dream visited me. It had a nightmarish quality about it. I found myself standing in a graveyard with hundreds of women, perhaps thousands, who had stood up out of their coffins crying and holding up their hands that were bound by chains. They were women in my family lineage. The dust of the world was upon them and they begged for release.

When I spoke to Howard, he was not surprised but simply said it was time to release my lineage through his prayers. His "Concise Formula of Prayer" program had long been part of my daily practice, but speaking the words with him then, I felt a rush of wind and an intelligent light that released all the women from their chains.

Howard asked again if I was ready to know the Light

and I said with passion that I was ready. We were just two people talking on the phone having what seemed to be a normal conversation when he opened the doors to the Infinite Light. I am not quite sure what he did exactly, but it felt as though a portal opened within and around me. I was suddenly inside a funnel of light. I could feel strands pulling at me as though I was in a wind tunnel and could hear voices that seemed to be located in my belly area or solar plexus. Images opened up before me like a television screen. I watched several scenes of family members speaking. Some of the people I recognized and others I did not. A few of the conversations were angry, but most seemed very loving. I had the intuitive understanding that I was made in the image of my grandmothers and grandfathers who had come before me. I was having the experience of being created out of the words and thoughts of my lineage. I realized I was the love, the hope and the suffering of ancestors who lived on inside of me.

Howard spoke to me and it seemed as though I could speak down the tunnel. Many people were listening, but I could not distinguish between those who were physical and those who were in spirit. He asked me again if I wanted to know the Infinite Light. As soon as I said yes my body began to quake. Knowing that my body needed to be protected, I crawled down the hall and climbed into bed. My husband was with me observing and witnessing what was occurring. My body was quaking again and weakened from the amount of Light that was streaming in. Another cosmic door opened in front of me and a brilliant light shone forth. It seemed to simultaneously shine before me and within me. The touch of the Divine Light made my body crumple, and I knew that I was losing connection with my physical form. I was not frightened, for I had experienced light activations strong enough to make me faint before. As I lay in my bed, I could smell the fragrance of roses that seemed to be pouring like essential oils through my skin.

A portal of light had now opened enough to allow me to go through. It was clear that my body was lying on the bed and I was to move without my form. My spirit lifted up like a mist or vapor with ribbons of pale colors within it. Everything that I considered "me" came with my misty spirit. Strings like energetic umbilical cords were attached to my energy field. I felt at peace with my husband, who was meditating near my body, and my children were busy with school and friends. But I felt a tug from my parents as though they did not want me to go and I was also aware of my deep love for them. My attachment to them had pulled me to earth as a baby and to leave I had to let go of my connection with them. For some reason that was my greatest struggle, but my desire to end illusion and know God was stronger and so I consciously laid the life cords to my parents aside and in that moment I began to sense a strong cosmic pulse.

I felt the limitations of my personality self begin to melt. For a moment I feared what might happen if there was no identity, but as I expanded outwards, the ego identity became an object to be discarded like a ripe cornhusk that was gently shucked away by a great intelligence. I was aware of my judgments, conflicts, and misdeeds as they played in little whirlpools like videos all around and within me. Although I felt some regret, the overriding feeling was love, compassion, and acceptance for all that had taken place in my life.

For a while I could speak with Howard, some friends who were listening and my husband, but as I went further it felt as if I was disappearing under water and communication lines began to shut down. Perhaps my mind would not rationally process what was occurring. As my limited self with all of its stories, concerns, and goals dissolved, I became aware of the loving intelligence of which I am a part. I merged with it one layer at a time, expanding outward like ripples in a vast sea. This level was attuned with the intelligence of the natural world, and I observed the consciousness of the invisible rainbow essence that understands and cares for all sentient beings. It tends all flowers, trees, animals, meadows, mountains, lakes, skies, and oceans. This vast intelligence lovingly nurtures and witnesses the birth, unfolding, and death of its creations. A perfection is at work in the cycles of all of evolution that is gentle and loving, yet also dynamic and final. You cannot argue with it. I saw that we are all biological programs that simply play out our lives like robots unless we awaken to what is real; and even then there is an organic process that our bodies adhere to. We needn't be frightened by it, for we are always cared for beyond belief.

The biological program of my body/mind melted and what was left of my soul flowed with the warm perfumed currents gently surrounding me. I relaxed into the ever-widening streams. Floating in eternal cosmic reality where time and space has collapsed into nothingness, I was encircled by living stars and galaxies. I could sense how the pulse of the stars attuned with my thoughts and put into motion manifestations of reality. What we speak and think creates the lives that we live into. I could see how prayers and positive words empower us.

At this point I sensed a pressure and felt an even greater need to surrender as my self-image and the sinews of the remaining body/mind complex further dissolved. I felt some resistance, for I realized I was familiar with my specific orientation and life history. I liked myself and wanted to care for this self, as one would care for a loved pet. I felt fleeting sorrow for not wholly understanding my inner femininity. I had not truly understood what a blessing motherhood can be, or how valuable each detail in our lives really is. From this perspective every breath seemed like a gift; each cup of tea made with a friend, every word that had ever been exchanged had value and meaning. It became clear that there was no goal or mission beyond growing in consciousness and then sharing what we have learned with others, for nothing else is required of us. I was told, but not by words so much as an inner knowing, that I could write about these mysteries, for the act would help others find their way.

Then I entered a vast silence, followed by a big bang that echoed throughout time and space—until there was only the eternal now. The small self had melted back with an immeasurable loving intelligence that knew every thought of every human, every cell and piece of grass and every galaxy in space simultaneously. From this perspective of infinite loving intelligence emerged a great peaceful stillness and an active dynamism that instructed life. God was neutral, loving, and kind.

There are universal laws that govern all things and it is in our favor to work in alignment with these guidelines. I saw that if we live by the laws of life, our lives go well and if we go against the laws we suffer. It's that simple. We have free will, so we make the choices and reap the rewards. We need to turn our face to God, love ourselves, and love one another. That's our practice.

When people steal, they steal from themselves; when they lie, they stain themselves; when they engage in sexual misconduct, they bind themselves to suffering. The Light is neutral about all of this, but the law is exact. There is no judgment but a precise pulse that informs life through our thoughts, words, and deeds. Planet Earth and human beings are greatly supported and loved. We are simply children growing up.

Merged in the cosmic ocean of consciousness, there resides the peace of an ideal meditation. The order of the universe is impeccable and we all have a perfect place within it. We are already forgiven, because creation simply wishes for us to discover the qualities and capacities of our true nature.

Although I had no sense of time in the eternal now, three days had passed on earth. There was no self to experience the time/space continuum. Howard told John Patrick that it was time to feed me meat, specifically lamb, so that I would come back into my body. There was no desire left to live or die, but simply to reside in the immensity of All That Is. I had little regard for my body, and I had to make a very conscious shift back toward form. The intimate connections that we have with others keep us healthy and curious about life. I'm usually vegetarian, so the cooked lamb was a shock to my system. I immediately sensed a contraction. The cube of meat tasted like death and began to pull me out of my unity-merge. The contractions began like a mother giving birth, squeezing an enormous essence into a tiny form. I felt a sonic boom from the pressure waves of sound and energy vibrations compressing and individualizing.

I re-entered through waves of color and musical tones back into a tightly contained environment. My body/mind complex seemed too small and I heard cracks and pops as my spirit slipped back into my body. My hips and legs ached from the lack of movement and I almost regretted returning until I opened my eyes and saw John Patrick looking at me with such devotion, tenderness, and love. A thrill came to mind accompanied with a shudder as I remembered my cosmic playmate. I felt the cords of love extending from my parents, sisters, and children, and allowed them to reform a life-affirming pattern. It was okay to focus on this world; indeed, it was wonderful to be back with clearer vision. I returned knowing that each moment is precious and that all of us have a place in existence that is specifically designed for us, whether we know it or not. Each and every one of us is a beautiful mandala, perfectly living out the lessons we have come here to learn.

I have written daily since that time, not because I have to but because I love to. It's my bliss. When I write I connect back to the Infinite Light that leads, guides, directs, and protects all of us who wish it. There is much I cannot yet describe because I do not have a vocabulary for it. Also the sequences in the experience followed a spiral, not a linear, route, so cosmic events can seem paradoxical or even irrational and so are difficult to share. Perhaps that is why many people choose to keep their experiences to themselves.

Integrating over the next few weeks was challenging. I had to crawl like a baby at first, learn to be gentle with myself and simply take my time. I wrote these poems and prayers as a way of integrating the living rainbow, as well as the new spaces and dimensions that had revealed themselves to me. Now I offer them to you as a transmission of Light, as a reminder that we are eternal beings having a brief adventure here on earth. There is nothing to fear, and much to love. We are all connected to a greater Light that loves us beyond belief.

Many people have told me that they have also had light activations while reading these words. Maria Cristina has been inspired to sing some of the poetry in this book. It always warms my heart when I hear stories of people who have had been touched in positive and life affirming ways.

The Light is always with me now, and so is my humanness. My husband shares a field of loving, which is not separate from me, for we are one wave moving together in an immaculate field of consciousness. When we merge in inquiry or meditation there is only one uni-body, a multi-faceted diamond that contains myself, my husband, and God: one cosmic spaceship that can experience a locality or can merge with the totality and be at peace with the luminous emptiness. Moved now by the dynamism of creation to write these words, I know there is only one focus and that is to be fully present, to love ourselves and each other, and to be at peace with all things. Then our lives are a blessing and all of creation is filled with our loving-kindness. It is our time to serve as intelligent and loving stewards of the earth. I love you; thank you for loving me.

The Mystical Light

When we call upon the Light which is found in all the natural elements and the sounds that are found deep in the forest and along rushing streams, we may taste the beyond for a moment. The Infinite Light sustains us like the invisible warming rays of the sun. The flow of the tones and colors I witnessed and merged with during my three days in the Light are echoed here in this book. These words and images are designed to help us glimpse something of the beauty beyond the veil of normal human awareness. The pages reflect the mystical rainbow that I saw during my journey Home. This is an attempt to share a taste of the experience. Reading the words or hearing others speak or sing the poetry helps remind me of the Infinite Light. Many people have shared that these pages have opened the doors to their own mystical experiences. I hope this is true for you also.

1
Vast Embrace

Please Hold Me

Mother Father God, Infinite One
Please Help Me Remember Who I Am
Please Lead Me From Darkness
To The Truth Of Who I Am
Please Hold Me And Accept Me
Until I Remember That I Am Love
Thank You

I Am Love

Infinite One
Please Help Me Recall
Your Warm And Tender Embrace
In The Moments When I Forget Who I Am
Please Whisper Messages To Me
So That I May Remember
That I Am Love
Thank you

May I Play Again

I Wish To Free All That Waits Within Me To Be Born
May My Limitations Be Washed Away
By A Silent River
May I Play Again
As A Child In The Ebbing And Flowing
Currents Of Existence
I Open My Mouth To Sing
Yet Feel Ashamed For An Instant
Who Am I To Have Such A Great Longing?
Please Forgive Me
But I Wish To Write This Opera
I Want To Know My Own Life
And How To Move With It
I Yearn To Know God's Immensity
And How To Mirror It
Without Shattering
I Sense That Where I Am Closed And Tight
I Am Yet Untrue
I Want To Unfurl
So That No Blossom Within Me
Is Fruitless Or Withered
And No Song Is Left Unsung

I Love My Life

I
LOVE
I LOVE MY LIFE
I LOVE MY LIFE
I LOVE MY LIFE
I LOVE
I
AM
LOVE
I LOVE YOU
I LOVE YOU
I LOVE YOU
THANK YOU
FOR LOVING
ME

Your Magnitude

Everything I Say, Write Or Paint
Can Be Eclipsed By Your Presence
We Spend Time Naming Things
Yet You Take The Words Back
Into The Great Silence
I Want To Love All Of Creation
As It Is Right Now
This Small Form Is Breaking
Beneath Your Magnitude
Please Hold Me
While You Are Writing

2
Myself in You

Myself in You

Please Allow Me To See Myself In You
That I May Remember We Are One
Please May I Love All People
And May All Of Creation Love Me
So That Grace Fills My Days
May Our Prayers Of Wholeness
And Restoration Be Answered
Thank You

Let's Live Together

This Prayer Is For All The People Of The World
May We Awaken Together
May We Remember Who We Are
Why We Are Here
And How To Live Together
May We Be Sensitive To The Needs Of The Earth
And The Vulnerability Of The Living Oceans
May We Remember How To Attune
To All Sentient Beings
For The World Is Alive
May We Remember That Together
We Create Solutions
That Bring Solace To The World
May We Remember That Together We Are Fulfilled

The Cosmic Couple

Magnificent Creator
Please Teach Me The Ways Of Healthy Sexuality
Show Me How To Honor Life
And The Union Of Lovers
For Even When I Am Alone
The Dance Of The Cosmic Couple Is Within Me
Please Use Your Divine Light
To Burn Away All Patterns That Prohibit
Pure Pleasure Within My Body
Please Remove The Desire To Dominate
Or Be Dominated
And All Tendencies Towards Harm Or Victimization
Restore The Patterns That Support The Play of Ecstasy
Creation, Please Teach Me How To Embrace The Beloved
So That I May Truly Live and Thrive
And Experience The Full Pleasure Of Life
Thank You

Yes and No

Infinite Light
Please Help Me Feel
When To Honor My YES
And Also Support Me
When I Need To Say NO
And Choose Again
Please Help Me Stand Up For Myself
Thank You

Life is Giving Birth to Me

Life Is Giving Birth To Me
And I Delight In The Journey
I Create To Remain Free
I Am Free To Create
I Live As My Authentic Self
And Life Is Always
Going On Around Me

The Artesian Well

Great Spirit
Please Teach Me To Access Creative Energies
Help Clear Away What Does Not Serve My Life
So That Inspiration Can Flow
From The Artesian Well
That Is My True Nature
Thank You

3
Illumination

Unquenchable Spiritual Fire

Infinite Self
Please Remind Me That I Am
Like The Gods And Goddesses Of Ancient Days
I Have What It Takes To Pass The Initiations
Of Both Matter And Spirit
As Your Instrument
I Am A Hero Or Heroine
Who Can Overcome All Obstacles
An Ancient Spirit Who Can
Melt Into Cosmic Bliss
And The Oneness Of Existence
Please Teach Me To Trust
So That I May Know Both Form And The Formless
Encase Me In Your Unquenchable Spiritual Fire
Amen

Unexpected Places

Dear Lord
There Are Times
When I Find Myself
In Unexpected Places
Please Lead Me And Guide Me
Towards You Always
And May I Be Forgiven
For Any Errors I Have Made
In My Forgetfulness
Thank You

Illumination

Arising At Dawn
The Sun Illuminates The Mountains
Sending Its Light Across Vast Oceans
The Bird's Chorus Reminds Us
Of The Sun Or Brilliant Star
That Resides Within Our Being
For Fifteen Billion Years
This Star Has Remained Unchanged
One Incarnation After Another
Each Day The Gold
Reveals The Gift Of Life

The Reminiscence

Infinite One
Please May I Remember
My Brilliancy
For I Truly Shine
I Am Magnificent
Assist Me And Evoke
Who I Am
For In The Reminiscence
I Also Remember You
Amen

Joy

Grant Me The Freedom
To Express My Joy
Here And Now
Amen

The Star

Radiant One
Please Help Me Remember The Star
That Resides In The Center Of My Being
For This Is My Connection To You
And All Of The Brilliancy Of Existence
Please Bring Into My Mind
The Understanding And Deep Wisdom
That All People Are Celestial Beings
Walking In This Plane Of Existence
Some Have Forgotten Their Way
And Others Recall Who They Are
Assist Me In Seeing Myself And All People Clearly
For In Truth We Are All Shining Suns
Thank You

Love Song

I Have Been Knocking On All The Doors
In The Village Looking For You
And I Have Been Exploring All The Stars In Heaven
Calling Out Your Name
I Wish To Be A Torchbearer For Your Infinite Flame
Please Expose Me To Your Inner Sun
So That I May Be Illuminated By You
Fill Me With Your Grace
That I May Be A Light Upon This World
I Am A Flute Waiting To Be Played By You
Please Use Me
In Your Next Love Song

4

My Sacred Other

Empower Me

Infinite One
Please Lead Me And Guide Me
Through This World
Do Not Let Me Become Lost In Delusions
No Matter How Interesting They May Seem
Please Help Me Continue To Walk Towards
The Light of My True Self
With What Empowers Me By My Side
And Please May I Turn Away
From All That May Harm Me
Or My Friends And Family
May My Focus Be On Awakening
And May I Always Know My Way
Amen

The Heart of All Living Things

Compassionate One
Please Help Me Awaken To The Loving
Intelligence Of All That Is
I Ask To Attune
The Pulse Of My Heart
With The Heart Of All Living Things
Beloved One
Please Show Me How The Visible
And The Invisible Worlds Interweave
In The Co-Creation Of Life
Through Your Infinite Loving Presence
Please Allow Me To Know
That We Are One
Thank You

Sharing My Heart

Infinite One
Please Assist Me In Awakening To Love
As My Heart Opens With Compassion
I Realize That I Need Nothing
I Am Complete As I Am
Yet I Would Like To Share My Heart
With Someone Special
Who Is My Perfect Mirror
That We May Know Each Other More Fully
Please Guide My Perception
So That We May Overflow With Your Nectar
And In Our Melting
Know Ourselves As One
Amen

My Sacred Other

Dear Infinite One
Please Send Me My Beloved
So That I May Delight
With My Sacred Other
Please Hold Us In Grace
And Compassionate Wisdom
Thank You

Open My Heart

Infinite Self
Please Give Me The Courage
To Turn The Key Within The Star Of Your Heart
So I May See Deeply Inside Myself
Looking Into My Mirror Of Truth
Which Reflects Light And Beauty
Help Me To Forgive And Let Go
Releasing Stories Of The Past
That No Longer Serve Me
So That I May Open Fully And Completely
To My True Nature
May I Remember Who I AM
For When I Express From My Essence
I Live Ecstatically In Joy
Please Open My Higher Heart
That I May Know Love And Bliss
And Find Liberation
In Loving Another
Amen

5

The Unbridled Self

The Unbridled Self

Infinite One
Please Be With Us Until We Realize You Fully
Let Us Know Of Your Creative Intelligence
We Are Not Afraid For Our Hearts Tell Us
That Presence Is The Source Of All Goodness
The Rest Is Only Illusion

May All Of The Natural World
All People Of The Earth
And All Star-Beings Throughout The Cosmos
Be Abundantly Cared For In Each Moment
May We Change Any Thoughts Or Ideas That Limits Us
Assist Others Who Also Wish To Transform
And Trust That All Sentient Beings Are Cared For
Perfectly Wherever They May Be
In Their Evolution

May We Meet The Unbridled Self
Who Swims In The Ocean Of Compassion
And Unbounded Love
May We Know The Wealth Of The Truth
Our True Prosperity
May We Become Fully Aware Of Your Loving Presence
And Know Without Hesitation
That There Is No True Separation
That Exists Between Us
Thank You

Immunity Prayer

Infinite Light
Please Sing A Song For My Immune System
So That I Am Protected All The Days Of My Life
May Illness Run From Me
When I Feel A Shadow Cross My Heart
Remind Me To Return To You
For In That Moment
With Your Grace I Am Healed
Be With Me Always
Especially In Times Of Sorrow
Help Me Look Outside Of Myself Once Again
And Rejoice In All Of Your Creations
Amen

My Closest Friend

All That Is
Please Hold Me In Your Presence
And Open Up My Guidance
So That I May Walk With You
And Speak With You
Please Be My Closest Friend
Open My Consciousness
So That I Am Flooded In The Starlight
With Your Perception
May Our Eyes Be As One Eye
And The Steady Pulse In My Brow
Be A Reminder
That You Are Always With Me
Amen

Blue

I Look Up And Behold The Open Expanse
Of The Daytime Sky
The Blue Surrounding Me
Initiates The Design
Of Perfect Health
Peace And Protection

Blue Opens The Doorway To New Life
And One Day, The Doorway Out

Blue, The Undifferentiated Oneness Of Blue
Fills Me With Tranquility
I Become Immersed In Blue
Until The 'I' Is
Absorbed By Consciousness

Merging With Blue
Means Knowing Gasses And Atoms
In The Blue State Of Oneness
Divine Origins Bloom

To My Mother and Father
I Love You

To My Mother And Father
I Love You
In My Eyes You Are Flawless
I Release All Judgments I Have Held
In This Lifetime Or Any Other Lifetime
You Have Done The Best Job Possible
Thank You For Giving Me My Life
I Release You From Your Duty
And I Continue To Love You
May You Always Be Held
In The Light

I Love Myself
May My Body Be Filled With
Sweetness
And My Mind Be Illuminated With Truth
I Forgive Myself For Any Delusions
I Was Once Entangled In
Or Beliefs That My Ancestors
Mistakenly Believed To Be
True
I Set Myself Free

I Know That The Light
Has Always Been With Me
And I Am Part Of That Light

There Has Never Been An Instance
When I Was Not Loved
For The Truth Is
I Am Love
We All Are Love

We Are Divine Beings
Having An Experience Of Earth
We Have All Been Learning Together
There Has Never Been A Time When We Were Separate
From What Is Good And True
Although We Might Have Thought It
The Heart Knows The Full Union
Of Existence

My Mind Is Now In Service
To My Heart
The Truth, The Love And The Light
Have Set Me Free
Have Set Us All Free
If We Wish It

God I Ask
For Release Now
May I Be Taken And Transformed
In The Luminous Blue Light
Of The Divine

Thank You

6

Like A Gentle River

A Lotus Blossom

Infinite Spirit
May Our Thoughts Be Attuned With All Of Creation
Please Guide Us In Awakening
From The Dream Of The Unreal
Into The Truth Of Eternal Wisdom
Help Us Remember Our Inner Star
That Never Dies Or Diminishes
But Moves From Lifetime To Lifetime
Without Changing
Please Take What No Longer Serves Us
Back Into The Light And May We Return To Peace
Please Inspire Our Lips
So That Our Words Are In Harmony
With All Of Existence
Please Reveal Your Divine Wisdom
Leading Us From Ignorance Into Divine Intelligence
Please Reveal Yourself To Us
Infinite Spirit
We Invite Your Vastness
To Open Our Consciousness Like A Lotus Blossom
We Are Ripe For Your Kiss

Take Me As Your Child

Please Protect And Guide Me
That I May Be An Instrument Of Peace
Show Me How To Surrender To Divine Wisdom
So That I May Understand
And Participate In The Perfect
Unfoldment Of Life
Please Support Me As I Dissolve Into Essence
And Remember Who I Am
May You Hold Me With Love As I Return To You
Please Take Me As Your Child
And Care For Me
Thank You

The Cosmic Dance

Infinite Light
Please Open The Doorway To Divine Knowing
So That I May Be Attuned And Dance
With The Creations Of Life
And Play In This Realm
Like The Gods And Goddesses Who Never Fell
May All Of My Seven Senses Open
And May I Thoroughly Enjoy My Life
In This Freedom May I Be
A Steward And Caretaker
Of This Garden Called Earth
May The Mother Shield Me With Her Protection
And The Father Lead
And Guide Me With Inner Light
Please May I Be A Loving Presence
Now And Forever

Great Spirit

Great Spirit
I Wish To Forgive And Release All People I Have Judged
Or Condemned Even Those Who Have
Tried To Dominate The Indigenous Peoples
The Healers And Wisdom Keepers
All The Light Bearers Who Had To Hide
Their True Natures
I See
The People Of The Earth
Fell Asleep For A While
And Now I Hear Them Waking
Please Forgive Me For Forgetting This Is A Dream
Help Me Remember This Upon Waking
Thank you

May the Light Be Kindled

Dear God,
May The Light Within Be Kindled
Please May I Carry The Unquenchable Fire
Of Goodness And Healing Wherever I Go
May This Gift Never Be Forgotten
And May It Be Shared With All
Who Wish To Receive
The Infinite Light,
Amen

Like a Gentle River

Infinite Self
May The Light Pour Upon Me
Like A Gentle River
Awakening Me From This World Of Dreams
May I Remember The Truth
Please
Transform Me With Love and Grace
Allowing My Body To Be Filled With Divine Light
Please Soothe Me
And Restore Me
So That I May Know What It Is Like
To Be Liberated From The Small Self
And Know What It Means To Live
In Heaven On Earth
Amen

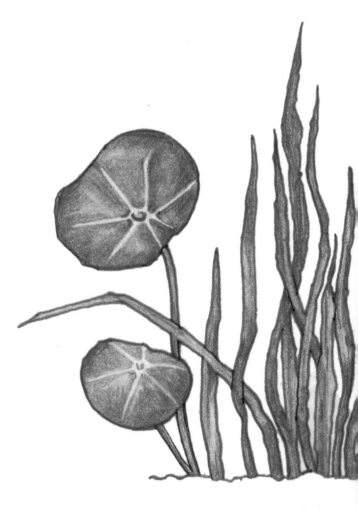

7
I Am That

The Tiny Grasses

God, I Love You
And Creatures Of All Shapes And Sizes
I Am Remembering
To Love The Smallest Things
The Tiny Grasses
The Details Of The Flowers
The Smiles On Children's Lips
And Observe That The Whole World
Is Supported In Its Unfolding

Uplift Me

Dear Infinite One
Thank You For Loving Me
This World That I See Today
Is Truly Magnificent
Thank You For Uplifting Me
So I Can See The Truth Again

I Am That

God
Infinite Clear White Light
I Drop The Garments Of The World
From My Body, Mind And Soul
So That I May Walk As A Child
In Your Garden Once Again
Please Fill Me With Your Grace
Hold Me, Love Me And Protect Me
On The Journey Home
Back Into Your Heart
May I Never Lose My Way Again
But Surrender Fully Into The Bliss Of Being
Let Me Taste The Truth Of Infinity
And Know Everlasting Life
I Am That
I Am
Thank You

Clearing the Veil

Divine Light
Please Clear The Veil Of Separation
So That I May Experience
The Full Radiance Of Your Being
Please Expose My True Nature
Melting Suffering, Pain And Ignorance
Revealing The Essences
Of The Universal Colors Of Love

I Revel In The Cosmic Dance Of Light
And Play On This Earth
I Am Open
Free And Radiant

Thank You

Mending the Rainbow Bridge

Infinite Light Please Help Me
End The Dualism Within Me Now And Forevermore
And Guide Me To Be Neutral, Loving And Kind
Please Forgive Me And All Of My Family Members
All Of Our Ancestors And All Their Relationships
Back Through All Time, Space And Dimension
Through All Of Our Lifetimes On Earth
And In Other Galaxies And Dimensions
Please Forgive Us For Any Ways In Which
We Have Been Out Of Touch And Misaligned
With The Truth Of Who We Are
Help Us Forgive and Release Ourselves
All The Way Back To Our Origin
In The Beginning Of Time
Divine Light

Please Help Us All
Compassionately Forgive Ourselves
So That Our Hearts May Open
Our Minds Be At Peace
And Our Bodies Be Made Healthy And Well
In The Image Of Our Divine Blue Print
May We Learn To Be As You
And Create Paradise Here On Earth

I Humbly Ask That We Are All Released
From Our Falsehoods
And Misinterpretations Of Reality
May We Be Filled With The Light Of Your Love

Please Touch Us With Complete Peace
Beyond Understanding
That Knows No Disturbance
May We Live In Peace Now And Forever
Please Help Us Know
That There Is Never A Separation From You
The Origin Of Love, Peace, Goodness, Beauty,
Creativity, Health, Bounty, Abundance And Wisdom
Please Lord
May We Become More Like You

We Thank You For Restoring Us With Love
And Transforming Us Like A Star Or Sun
Filling Us With Eternal Light
We Thank You For Goodness And Peace
May We Be Remade In Your Image

May The Connection Between Myself
And All Of My Ancestors
Be One Filled With Love, Light And Goodness
Please Let All Sorrows Melt Into The Cosmos
May My Ancestral Lineage
All Of Our Spouses And Children
Both Born And Unborn
Be Harmoniously Connected To The Sun,
To The Light, To God
May Only What Is True Remain
May My Ancestral Lineage Both In The Past
And In The Future
Be Connected To God
Now And Forever

May We Be Forever Liberated By The Light
Thank You

The Colors of Love

Beloved
You Have Held Me
Until It Is Certain That I Am Love
As My Heart Opens
I Become A Luminous Galaxy Within You
At Daybreak When The Birds
Begin Their Morning Chorus
I Call Out Your Name And For A Moment
I See Your Face In All Of Creation
There Is No Separation Between Us
Every Mountain And River
Overflows With Nectar
And The Skies Are Filled
With The Colors Of Love